Dedicated to:
Sarah and Lucy
Lauren and Josephine
Olivia Rubai
Atieno Carol

*With special thanks for research assistance
and technical guidance to*

Rod Salm
Coordinator, East African Marine Programme
The World Conservation Union

Mike Bess
International Conservation Specialist

Illustrations by George W. Kimani and Samwel Ngoje
Text by Bridget King and Susan Salm
Graphic Design by Katherine Mamai

All rights reserved. No part of this publication may be reproduced, stored in a retrieval system or transmitted, in any form or by means, electronic, mechanical, photocopying or otherwise, without prior written permission of the publisher.

First Published 1994

Text and illustration copyright (c) by Jacaranda Designs Limited
Original concepts by G. A. Porter and J. Okello.

Published by: **JACARANDA DESIGNS LIMITED**
P. O. Box 76691, Nairobi, Kenya

Typeset in Avant Garde, Palatino and CgDomcasualBd.
Developed and designed in Kenya. Printed in Singapore.

ISBN 9966-884-49-1

Introduction

This book offers hilarious illustrations along with some wonderful facts about the ocean. As a fun *and* educational book, it introduces young children to the wonders and importance of the earth's vast bodies of water, and the many creatures that live in them. This book has been developed in the interest of marine conservation, worldwide.

It is significant in conservation education for a child to think of our planet as a healthy human body. Instead of organs, the earth has important ecosystems that work together to keep the 'body' alive and well. Open oceans, grasslands, coral reefs, deserts, and mangrove forests are some of these different ecosystems. In each ecosystem, the plants and animals living there need each other to survive. If too many of these ecosystems are degraded, then the well-being of our earth is affected. Healthy ecosystems mean a healthy planet.

Focused on the East African coast and selected marine life of the Indian Ocean, this book introduces young children to some specific habitats. On this coast, there are as many remarkable and diverse ecosystems *along* the sea and *in* the sea, as there are on the land of Africa. And yet, we know so little about them. It's not easy to study the areas, plants and animals which live underwater, especially when some marine animals migrate thousands of kilometres! But, this is truly a rich and exciting frontier for our children to explore. For them to discover the magnificent wonders of our oceans may well set them on a fascinating journey, a journey to last their lifetime!

Hugo Hippo makes this a most lively introduction!

How to make the best use of this book

This book is designed for children of all ages to stimulate their love for science, and encourage their natural curiosity and imagination. It is not necessary to know the East African Coast to enjoy this book as many of the facts will apply to other coastal and marine ecosystems.

How to use this book:
Read the alliterative text aloud: *it has been specially written to sound fun!*

Look at the pictures and talk about all the different things you can see. Look out for Hugo's bird friend, *Professori* , who is always doing something a bit unusual and amusing!

Beneath the alliterative text you will find an information box. You may need to help your child to understand these interesting facts about the habitats and lifestyles of each creature. The drawings will help you to identify some of the wonderful things you can find on the beach, in rock pools or in the sea.

Hugo Hippo's
Fun Book at the East African Coast

Text by Bridget King and Susan Salm
Illustrated by George W. Kimani and Samwel Ngoje

Here's Hugo .....

...receiving a letter from Marta, his marine hippo cousin. She lives around the Bijagos Islands off the coast of Guinea Bissau.

Marta's letter tells Hugo how enjoyable life by the sea can be. Hugo is a fresh water hippo from a lake in Kenya. He has never been to the sea before, so he decides to visit the East African coast of the Indian Ocean.

Let's go with him!

Here's Hugo .....

sitting on the sand with sunhat, sunglasses and sunscreen.

Sand has been made over millions of years. Rocks, corals, dead seashells and animal skeletons have been broken down by the waves and ground into the tiny pieces that we call grains of sand.

When you visit the Indian Ocean, don't forget your **sunscreen, sunhat** and **sunglasses** to protect you from the very strong ultraviolet rays of the sun. Sunburn is bad for you!

Here's Hugo .....

singing
sea shanties
with a Swahili sailor.

> The **Swahili** coastline stretches from the Red Sea to Mozambique. The Swahili people are traditionally fishermen and traders and many of their ancestors came from Arabia.

Here's Hugo .....

dining deliciously with a dolphin on a dhow.

Dolphins are not fish, but warm blooded mammals that need to breathe air. They travel in groups and make sounds to communicate, are intelligent and easily trained. Some kinds of dolphins like to travel with tuna and as a result many have drowned in tuna fishing nets. Fishermen are now starting to use different nets that allow dolphins to escape. Many wonderful stories tell how dolphins have rescued people from danger.

A **dhow** is a boat used by Swahili and Arab traders for carrying cargo to and from the exotic ports of countries such as Kenya, Oman, Pakistan and Tanzania. Among other things, the traders carry Persian carpets, dates, henna, dried shark, carved wooden chests and mangrove poles.

Here's Hugo .....

filling jumbo jam jars with jolly jellyfish.

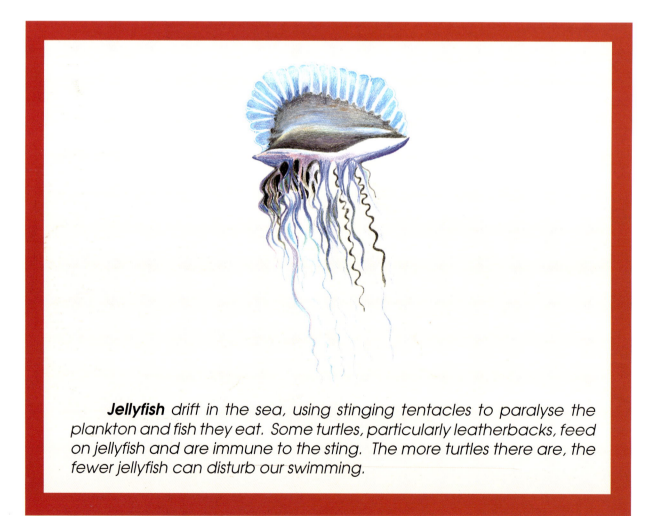

Jellyfish drift in the sea, using stinging tentacles to paralyse the plankton and fish they eat. Some turtles, particularly leatherbacks, feed on jellyfish and are immune to the sting. The more turtles there are, the fewer jellyfish can disturb our swimming.

Here's Hugo .....

lunching with a ladylike lobster and a looney lion fish.

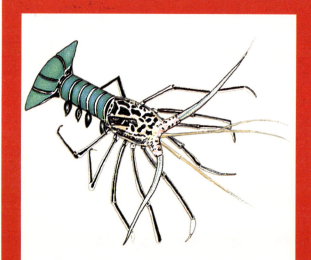

Lobsters' long antennae sometimes give them away as they hide in holes and crevices. Because they are so popular to eat, these crustaceans are often overfished and are becoming rare in some parts of the Indian Ocean.

Lion fish live amongst coral and dine on unsuspecting smaller fish as they swim past. Their beautiful colour pattern advertises that they are poisonous; their long spines are able to inflict painful wounds on predators that come too close.

Here's Hugo .....

making salt from sea water under a scorching sun.

Common **salt** is a mineral which once came from rocks. When sea water evaporates, the salt is left behind as tiny, white crystals. Some countries take the salt out of sea water to make fresh water. This is called desalination.

Here's Hugo .....

waving from a whale in the waves.

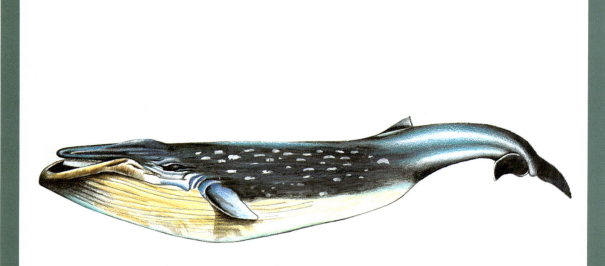

Whales *are large mammals that breathe air, give birth to live young and produce milk for their babies. They move through the water by moving their tails up and down, unlike fish which move them from side to side. As big as some whales are, many only feed on tiny marine animals called krill. Pollution, whaling and fishing nets have caused the death of so many whales that now the survival of many species is endangered.*

Waves *travel across the surface of the sea and most are caused by the wind. The greater the wind, the higher the waves. The power of the waves shapes the cliffs, wearing away the softer rock and creating bays, coves and caves.*

Here's Hugo .....

searching in the sand for shiny seashells.

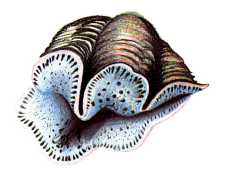

Bivalves are shells with two halves hinged at one end. Oysters, clams and scallops are examples of this type of shell.

Gastropods have just one shell which is usually coiled. These include cowries, cones and limpets. Colour taken from their food is used to pattern the shell.

Shells are molluscs and have soft bodies. Most molluscs are able to make a hard shell that provides protection. It's fine to collect dead shells on the beach, but not live ones from the sea as the animals inside will die. Shells fall into two groups: **bivalves** and **gastropods**.

Here's Hugo .....

cautiously cavorting with colourful crabs and other crustaceans.

*As **crabs** grow they get too big for their shells and moult. The shell splits and the crab climbs out. It blows itself up with water while a new shell is formed and hardens a few sizes bigger. While the shell is soft, the crab cannot run and can easily be attacked.*

Crustaceans *are a group of marine animals that include lobsters, crabs, prawns, shrimps and even barnacles. They have hard jointed outer skeletons, many legs and two pairs of feelers. Most crustaceans are very tasty!*

Here's Hugo .....

walking in the water with whelks and waders.

Whelks are a kind of shell. They are carnivorous and feed on other shells and marine worms. A whelk makes acid and uses it to soften a spot on a victim's shell, then drills a hole with its tongue to eat the soft body inside. If you find an empty shell on the beach with a single hole drilled through it, most likely it was a whelk's dinner.

Waders are long legged, slender billed birds which include snipes, curlews, sandpipers, plovers, rails and stilts. Snipes, curlews and sandpipers are often non-breeding visitors, spending their winters in Africa. Waders feed along the water's edge, sandy beaches and on mud flats and piles of seaweed or debris. Their nests are often made on the beach or grassland. Like many ground nesters, they have speckled eggs that help to camouflage them from foxes and other predators.

Here's Hugo .....

sampling slippery seaweed and sea cucumbers for a snack.

Sea cucumbers are sausage shaped animals that live on the ocean floor. Certain sea cucumbers are popular to eat in Asia. Sea cucumbers fight off predators by sending out sticky tubes from their gut, enveloping the predator and confusing it while the sea cucumber slowly moves away from danger.

Seaweeds are plants that anchor themselves to rocks or stones in the sea, creating food for themselves from sunlight and chemicals in the water. A slippery mucus covers some seaweeds, preventing the plants from catching on rocks as the waves push them about. Certain seaweeds are very nutritious.

Here's Hugo .....

cruising in a canoe above the coral reefs of Kenya.

*Although **coral reefs** resemble lovely gardens, corals are actually animals that need clean, clear water to live in. Coral reefs are very important feeding, breeding and resting areas for many kinds of fish. You should only look at coral and never touch it, step on it, or break pieces off as it damages very easily and can take many years to recover.*

Here's Hugo .....

making merry with a moray eel in a muddy mangrove.

A **moray eel** is a long snake-like fish with very strong teeth and jaws, which lives in crevices or holes during the day coming out at times to catch its prey.

Muddy **mangrove** swamps are extremely important feeding and breeding grounds for many fish, prawns and birds. Mangrove habitats play an important role in healthy fisheries as far as 50 kilometres away. Without mangroves, many fish and prawns would not survive.

Here's Hugo .....

observing an outsized octopus overeating oysters.

The octopus lives in pools and glides over rocks on eight suckered arms. It eat shells and crabs which are killed by its poisonous saliva. Its main predator is the moray eel. Octopus escape behind an inky cloud that they produce when predators come too close.

Rock Oysters have two very bumpy shells and live among other oysters on rocks at the edge of the sea. They are a popular seafood for many people. **Pearl oysters,** found in deeper water, have smoother shells and are known for the pearls that are sometimes found inside.

The **oyster** and the **octopus** are both molluscs but the octopus is one of the few molluscs without a shell.

Here's Hugo .....

getting to grips with a great green grouper.

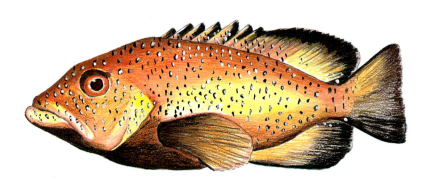

A **grouper** is a large fish also known as a rock cod. Fish breathe through their gills and have skeletons which support their bodies. Fish use their fins for movement, steering, braking and stabilizing. Unfortunately, groupers are easy to catch and are in danger of being eliminated from coral reefs.

Here's Hugo .....

discovering a wreck with a daring Digo diver.

*Being a **diver** is fun but you must be careful and use the right equipment. A wet suit keeps divers warm, tanks of air allow them to breathe under water and a special jacket enables divers to sink down in the water or rise back to the surface. Divers can study the underwater creatures in their own environment and sometimes they find sunken treasure!*

The Digo people live along the coastal region of Kenya.

Here's Hugo .....

sharing scary stories with scarlet starfish and sea urchins.

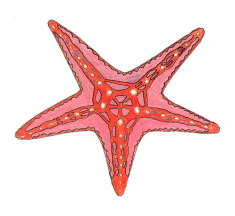

Starfish are not fish, but belong to the same family as sea urchins. On the underside of the starfish's five arms are rows of wriggling tube feet with suckers at their tips. These grip rocks and enable the starfish to move in any direction. Some starfish are able to regrow lost or damaged arms and sometimes a detached arm can grow into a whole new starfish! They feed on sea urchins, shells, coral and other starfish.

Sea Urchins have long slender spines that provide great protection from predators and people. A little fish even shelters amongst the spines for its own safety. Urchins have complicated jaws with five strong teeth that allow them to eat seaweeds and to scrape young plants off the rocks.

Here's Hugo .....

twisting with twin turtles as the tide turns.

Turtles swim great distances across the oceans, making it difficult to know just where they go and what they do. When the female is ready to mate, she returns to the beach where she was born and mates with a male turtle swimming just off the beach. When her eggs are ready, she slowly crawls up the beach and lays them in a hole that she digs in the sand. The turtle hatchlings must make their own way across the sand to the ocean and try to avoid the foxes, dogs, ghost crabs and gulls that feast on them.

Tides are caused by the sun and the moon as they regularly circle the earth, creating a pulling effect on the seas. This force results in the sea coming right up the beach at high tide and going out again at low tide.

Here's Hugo .....

smiling at sharks while snorkelling with a spotted stingray.

Most **sharks** need to swim continuously to take oxygen from the water as it flows over their gills. Contrary to belief, only a few of the 350 kinds of sharks are dangerous to people. The largest fish in the sea is the whale shark that feeds on tiny marine animals and plants as well as small fish and squid. Sharks act mainly by instinct and have poor eyesight with no colour vision. They have an excellent sense of smell and can accurately pinpoint vibrations in the water.

A **stingray** is a fish with a triangular shape and, like the shark, has a skeleton that is made of cartilage instead of bone. The stingray has a poisonous spine near the base of its whip-like tail. Stingrays like to lie partially buried in the sand.

Here's Hugo .....

happily angling with adorable adolescent angelfish.

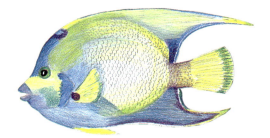

Like many coral reef fish, **angelfish** are territorial and their bright colours help them to recognise one another. The young fish are patterned differently so they aren't chased off the reef by the adults. As the young grow old enough to defend their territories and take care of themselves their colours change until they look like their parents.

Here's Hugo .....

having fun feeding french fries to friendly flying fish.

*Can **flying fish** really fly? No, but flying fish can escape predatory fish by jumping out of the water, spreading their fins and gliding for quite a distance before falling back into the sea.*

Here's Hugo .....

sipping a sundowner with seahorses and sleepy sea slugs.

The female **seahorse** lays her eggs in the male's pouch on his belly, where they remain until the young are fully developed. When the babies emerge, they are completely independent.
Seahorses are very well camouflaged in seaweed and use their tails to hold onto these underwater plants.

This tiny **pyjama nudibranch** is one of many really colourful sea slugs. Sea slugs are molluscs which lack a shell. They are protected from predators by their bright colours which advertise their foul taste!

East African Coast

DID YOU KNOW ?
SOME FUN FACTS ABOUT THE SEA

- The oldest life forms began in the oceans.

- The oceans and seas on our planet cover more than 70% of the earth's surface. Why then do we still call it Planet Earth?

- The Indian Ocean has 22% of the world's total sea area; Pacific Ocean 49%, Atlantic Ocean 25% and Arctic Ocean 4%. These are the earth's four oceans.

- The oceans play a very important part in the world's climate.

- In many countries, rubbish is loaded onto ships and dumped at sea. Rubbish thrown into the sea in Norway has washed up on the beaches of Texas!

- Vast amounts of human sewerage, industrial and urban waste also end up in our oceans. Scientists are still learning about how all these chemicals affect marine life.

- The ocean floor is not flat, but has mountains, volcanoes, vast plains and valleys (called trenches), just like on land. The Philippine Trench is 10,497 metres (34,441 ft) deep.

- One of the deepest known fish is the angler fish which lives in darkness at a depth of 4,000 metres or 13,600 ft.

- Sand dunes are stores of sand which replenish our beaches with sand after storms wash the beaches away.